OFFSHOOT

First edition 2017
Offshoot Books
An imprint of Kalabindu Enterprises Pvt. Ltd

GF–18, Virat Bhavan
Commercial Complex, Mukherjee Nagar
Delhi 110009
Phone: +91-11-47038000 / Fax: +91-11-47038099
Website: www.offshootbooks.com

Dear Reader,

Thank you for buying this book. We hope you enjoy every page of the book—and while you do that, please ensure that no one uses or transmits any part of this publication, in any form or by any means, without our prior written permission. You wouldn't want to offend the no-offence brand.

In case we haven't mentioned it before, we truly think that you are our favorite reader. Thanks for being a part of the Offshoot universe.

Have fun!

Love,
Team Offshoot

ISBN: 978-93-86362-38-4
Printed in India
Picture credits: www.shutterstock.com

WHAT WE THINK, IS WHO WE ARE,
OUR THOUGHTS BRING JOY OR MAKE A SCAR.
THINK HAPPY, IS WHAT WE PLEA—
FOR WHAT WE THINK, WE SHALL BE.

PANIC

Anything for which I am not ready,
makes me afraid, makes me crazy...

Why did you laugh, oh my sire?
Join the dots, that's a flat tire!

TELL YOURSELF!

I am calm. I have a serene and peaceful life.

Studied your best for the wrong test?
Work the maze to calm the unrest.

TELL YOURSELF!

I am smart. I am confident. I can manage this.

PHOBIA

Auditorium, joker or elevator,
you have caught me, no fear is greater…

…trapped in an elevator out of order,
doodle what you would feel—border to border.

TELL YOURSELF!

I am strong. I am in control. I can do anything.

People, people everywhere
and some jokers to be seen,
jokers give happiness to many
but I find them so mean.

FRUSTRATION

Bang your fist or bang your head,
all that is around only causes dread...

It is time to tip the balance of life,
match your joys with your strife.

All is well. I am at peace with myself.

TELL YOURSELF

When your mind has gone for a toss,
chart your feelings, you'll never be at a loss.

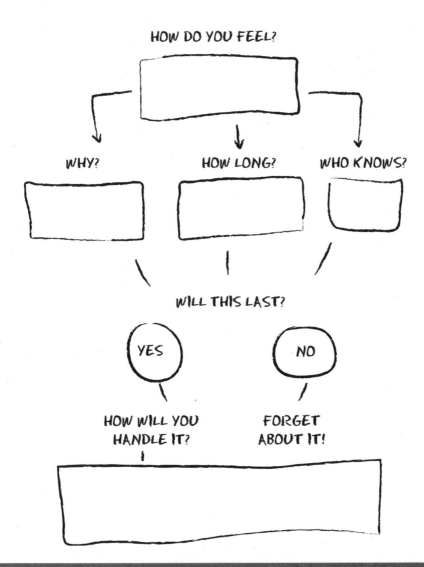

TELL YOURSELF!

I am different from others.
All of us are unique. All of us are right.

DEPRESSION

When nothing seems right, and everything is wrong,
when nothing you do, makes you strong...

Write down your worries, pen down your woes,
throw them away, as far as the bag goes.

What you feel,
tick the boxes to reveal.

- [ ] SAD
- [ ] MAD
- [ ] GLAD
- [ ] NICE
- [ ] NOT NICE
- [ ] JEALOUS
- [ ] PROUD
- [ ] GRUMPY
- [ ] JOYFUL
- [ ] STRESSED
- [ ] SLEEPY
- [ ] LAZY
- [ ] HUNGRY
- [ ] STARVED
- [ ] FRUSTRATED
- [ ] ANNOYED
- [ ] IGNORED
- [ ] IGNORANT

- [ ] STUCK
- [ ] FREE
- [ ] TIRED
- [ ] BORED
- [ ] APATHETIC
- [ ] PATHETIC
- [ ] HAPPY
- [ ] FRANTIC
- [ ] SLOW
- [ ] VERY SLOW
- [ ] LOVED
- [ ] HATRED
- [ ] CARELESS
- [ ] CAREFUL
- [ ] UNCERTAIN
- [ ] SURE
- [ ] SCARED
- [ ] POWERFUL

TELL YOURSELF!

I am strong. I love myself unconditionally.

STRESS

When worries take you for a ride,
and there is no relief on any side...

Paste pictures of things that make you feel good—
could be a person, a thing or any food.

TELL YOURSELF!
I am a positive thinker.
Nothing negative can ever affect me.

Life is a maze with highs and lows,
catch with glee, whatever life throws.

TELL YOURSELF!
All problems have a solution.
I can think and solve
all problems.

LOW SELF-ESTEEM

When the sky seems gray and the sun not bright,
when nothing you do seems too right...

Scribble some words for those rainy days,
to make you happy and enlighten your ways.

YOU ARE DOING IT RIGHT, HONESTLY. YOU GO, BUDDY!

TODAY IS A GOOD DAY! IT'S ONLY GOING TO BE BETTER.

THIS FEELS LIKE THE START OF SOMETHING GOOD!

I love myself. I accept myself, without any limitations or conditions.

TELL YOURSELF

Look into the mirror and trace your radiant,
bright and delightful face.

TELL YOURSELF!

I am unique. I am important.
I am loved and respected.

KNEE PAIN

The body aches and the joints creak,
every movement makes you shriek...

Join the dots and you will see,
you can be as healthy as you want to be.

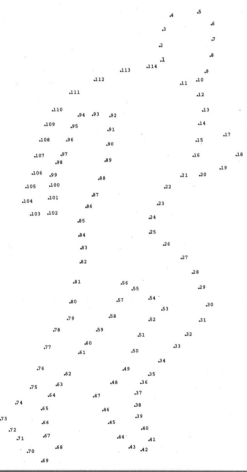

I release all stubbornness and ego that
I have stored in my knees.

TELL YOURSEL

Write about the incident that had brought so much pain.
If you overcome that hurt, your knee won't trouble you again.

ELL YOURSELF!

I release all stress and conflict that
I have stored in my knees.

17

LONELINESS

People around me are many,
but to call my own, I don't have any...

**Make this page your dearest friend,
write what you feel till the page ends.**

TELL YOURSELF!

I can feel the love and care of
the people who are no more with me.

Don't worry if you are on your own,
try as many of these—known or unknown.

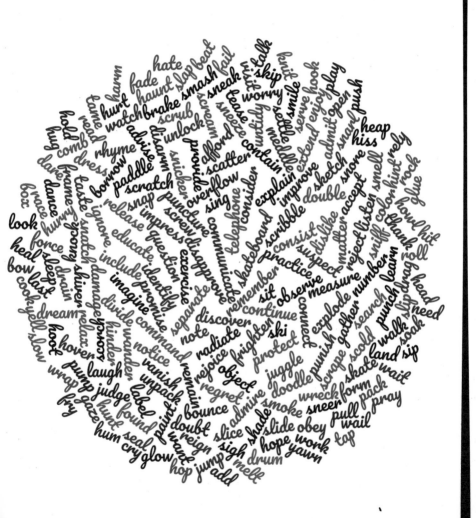

TELL YOURSELF!

I enjoy being on my own because I love myself.

FOOD POISONING

You couldn't digest whatever came your way,
your tummy threw out, what you couldn't say...

Make a list of all that will make,
a healthier you without any ache.

- ☐ **LOTS OF DRINKS**
- ☐ **TISSUES**
- ☐ **VITAMIN C**
- ☐ **A LITTLE SYMPATHY**
- ☐
- ☐
- ☐
- ☐
- ☐
- ☐
- ☐
- ☐

TELL YOURSELF!

I am powerful.
I am not defenceless.

20

Jot down the last four instances when your stomach failed to digest, and threw out everything in disgust.

21

NOSTALGIA

Bittersweet memories—a veil they cast,
slow you down and you dwell in the past...

Little moments you need to pin down,
the ones that made you laugh and not frown.

WE HIGH-FIVED

WE KISSED

YOU LAUGHED

I FELL DOWN

WE TALKED ALL NIGHT LONG

I am lucky, I have so much to be happy about!

TELL YOURSEL

Three of your most-frequent thoughts,

or what you wish they should have been, here you can jot.

_____

_____

_____

_____

_____

_____

TELL YOURSELF!

My thoughts don't make me, I make my thoughts. I am not going to let anything hold me back

ENNUI
(THE FEELING OF BEING ANNOYED)

When a heavy heart weighs you down,
steals your smile and brings a frown...

List the four times when you did try,
but each effort ended with a sigh.

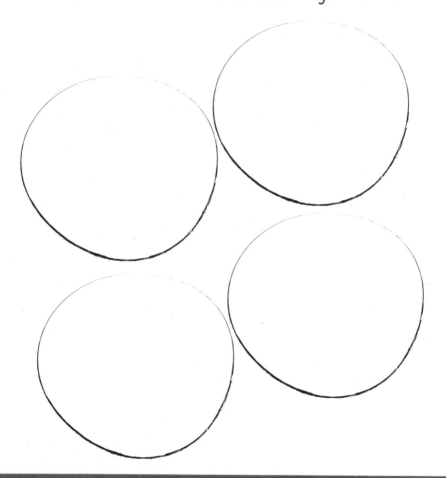

I choose to be at peace with myself.
No person or situation can annoy me.

TELL YOURSELF

Every time you tried to move ahead,
write the lesson learned in its stead.

FELINOPHOBIA

Why they scare me I don't know,
they stop me in my tracks and breathing low...

Fill the outlines of the cats of your biggest fears,
keep coloring till the last shadow clears.

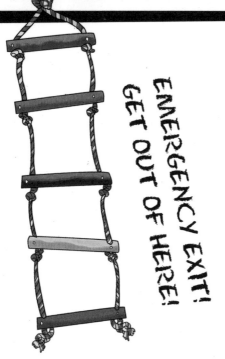

EMERGENCY EXIT!
GET OUT OF HERE!

Stuck in a room with a feline,
between dislike and fear, how did you manage to draw a line?

TELL YOURSELF!

I am my own hero. Nothing can scare me.

SEA SICKNESS

Fretful weather, an angry sea,
make you as sick, as sick you can be...

Write on a paper a secret you cherish,
the one that you don't want to perish.

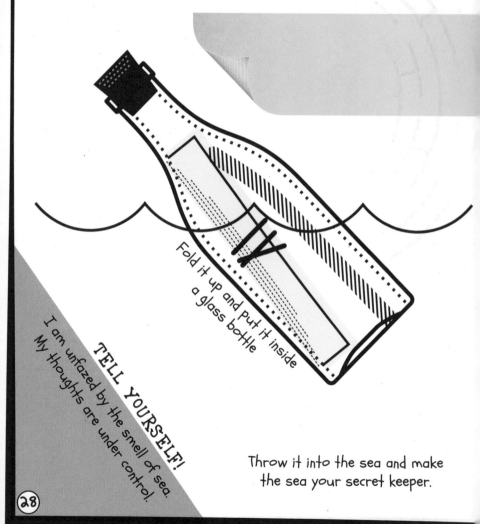

Fold it up and put it inside
a glass bottle

TELL YOURSELF!
I am unfazed by the smell of sea.
My thoughts are under control.

Throw it into the sea and make
the sea your secret keeper.

Through this maze that you can see,
make your way out of the sea.

TELL YOURSELF!
I am calm. I am at peace.
I can let go of my fear.

HYPERVENTILATION

Breath in and breath out,
faster and faster—

doodle while you face it,
to keep calm and feel better.

Learning yoga will give you the nerves of steel,
color this image—that's the deal!

TELL YOURSELF!

I trust the process. I trust the person. I can change.

SNORING

Pillows, nose clips, pegs—you tried them all,
you couldn't stop snoring, will it be your downfall?

Strong neck muscles take snoring away.
Sing to make your neck muscles strong,
write down your favorite lyrics, don't get them wrong.

When your partner snores through the night,
What are the thoughts you need to fight?

TELL YOURSELF!

It is safe for me to let go of old patterns. I don't need them.

33

ACNE

They appear when you are troubled, and trouble they brew,
cures and treatments—know of any, do you?

Some herbs can help in curing acne,
fill this crossword with their names, if you may.

ACROSS

4 NIOLDEDNA

5 EENRG EAT

7 DRE LVOERC

DOWN

1 NDEVAERL

2 MONLE ASSGR

3 OEAL REAV

6 EEMN

TELL YOURSELF!

I am gorgeous. I love myself. I am the best.

Four instances when you had an event coming up,
and with acne you woke up.

TELL YOURSELF!

I am beautiful. My skin is beautiful.
I have a clear skin.

35

ACHES

A discomfort of the body,
makes you act, oh so shoddy!

Of all the aches given here,
which ones do you have to bear?

Headache

Nasal Congestion

Ear Pain

Sore Mouth

Jaw Pain

Sore eye

Sore Throat

Heartache

Stomachache

Chest Pain

Finger Pain

Hand Pain

Arm Pain

Elbow Pain

Sore Butt

Backache

Hip Pain

Calf Pain

Knee Pain

Shin Pain

Toe Pain

Ankle Pain

Heel Pain

Foot Pain

To the doctor's surprise, this patient turned out very wise, what do you think did the doctor say, looking into his eyes?

PMS

Everything seems to be out of tune,
moods all over the place lie strewn...

Get rid of your anger, don't be bitter,
poke this page till you feel better.

TELL YOURSELF!

I am happy. I love myself. I love my cycles.

This pillow could be your comforter,
fill it with everything that makes you feel better.

TELL YOURSELF!

I am a woman. I love myself. I approve of myself.

ALCOHOLISM

Gave up on people, tired of life,
the bottle stands to end your strife...

Out of focus, without a care,
find the bottle without a pair.

I am free. Nothing has any power on me.
Nothing or no one controls me.

TELL YOURSELF

Draw lines with a free hand,
keep drawing them, till straight they stand.

I release my addiction. I have the power.
I am free.

INSOMNIA

Restful sleep eludes your eye,
peace and calm are put on standby...

The monster, Insomnia, is on your head,
color him bright, before you go to bed.

I will fall asleep quickly and
I will sleep soundly.

TELL YOURSEL
(just before y
go to bed

42

Make a playlist here,
of the best lullabies you care to share.

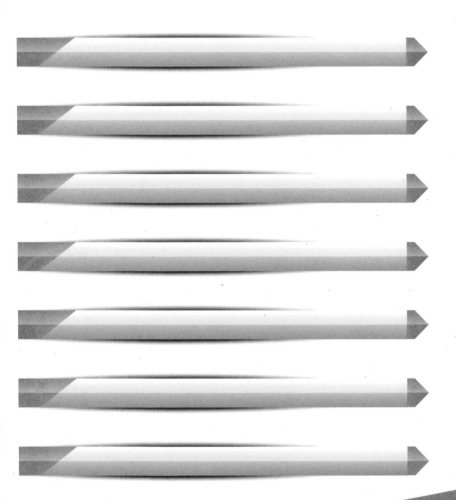

'ELL YOURSELF!
ist before you
go to bed)

I will sleep quickly and will let my body
rebuild and regenerate itself.

OBESITY

You eat and feel good and to feel good, you eat,
why not let everything else take a back seat?

Embrace yourself, bless your heart
while at it, make your weekly diet chart.

	Mon __/__	Tue' __/__	Wed __/__	Thu __/__	Fri __/__	Sat __/__	Sun __/__
BREAKFAST							
LUNCH							
DINNER							
NOTES							

TELL YOURSELF!

My body is healthy and fit. And so am I.

In this fitness word cloud,
mark the words that speak to you aloud.

TELL YOURSELF!

can control my eating habits. Every day I am reaching my ideal weight.

MIGRAINE

Your head will split, your head will break,
will someone end this dreadful ache?

The pounding in your head this picture will show,
if you join the pieces in one go.

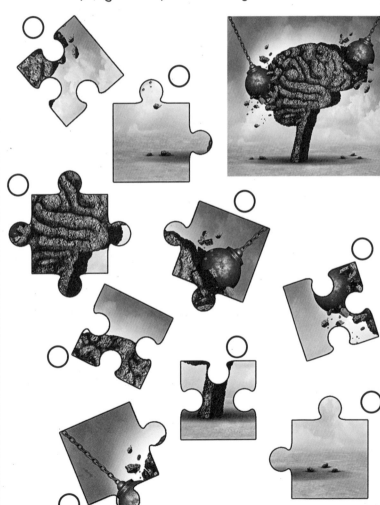

46

Make a list of things you have ready,
for the next time when your head might go unsteady.

o **ICE PACKS**

o **SUPPLEMENTS**

o **HERBS**

o

o

o

47

HYPERTENSION

A stressful lifestyle makes the blood throb in your vein,
pressure mounts and your peace is slain...

Choose and mark the ones that you'd do,
those that are sure to keep hypertension away from you.

SLOW DOWN

KEEP CALM

BE POSITIVE

UNPLUG

ENJOY LIFE

PEACEFUL SLEEP

BREATHE

RELAX

GO OUTSIDE

TAKE IT EASY

MEDITATE

TAKE GOOD DIET

Record your blood pressure levels regularly,
so that you can manage the pattern accordingly.

	Morning	Evening
mon		
tue		
wed		
thu		
fri		
sat		
sun		

notes
_____
_____
_____
_____
_____
_____

I am at peace with myself and the world. My future is open and full.

URINARY PROBLEMS

Burning sensations sear through you,
how to end it, if only you knew...

While in a dire emergency,
looking for a loo can be an act quite crazy.

TELL YOURSELF!
I release everything that has led to this condition. I am ready to change.

To fight out UTI, hydrate yourself well,
note every time you have water, here you can tell.

FROZEN SHOULDER

Whether it is this way or that,
turning your head is a difficult act...

Stretching can help your shoulder heal.
sketch a few stretching exercises and better you will feel.

I won't be stiff and allow my experiences
to be joyous and loving.

TELL YOURSEL

Arrange these postures in correct order,
the pain in your shoulder wouldn't be a bother.

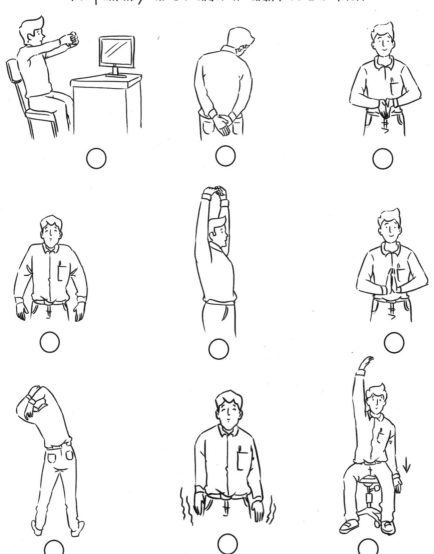

I won't lose my motivation and
will keep moving.

DENTAL ISSUES

They ache and they hurt,
they should be crystal white but they look full of dirt...

A strong decision you finally make,
and choose the right path the tooth should take.

TELL YOURSELF!

I am doing the right thing.
I am taking the right decisions.

Make a list of everything you want to be able to eat.

_____

_____

_____

_____

_____

_____

_____

Now, give each of your favorite food a name that will
remind you of the decisions you need to take.

_____

_____

_____

_____

_____

TELL YOURSELF!

I am not indecisive.

I will keep biting through the hardships of life.

DIABETES

Sugar levels in my blood are soaring high,
this has happened to me, but why?

Diabetic issues lie in line,
to each a correct place, you must assign.

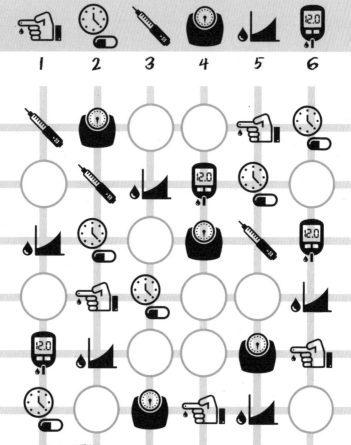

TELL YOURSELF!

It doesn't matter if I can't eat anything sweet,
I will dwell on the sweetness of life.

For high sugar levels I don't care,
till the people who give me these 🥛 are there.

HAPPINESS _____

LOVE _____

PEACE _____

COURAGE _____

FRIENDSHIP _____

STRENGTH _____

LAUGHTER _____

FAITH _____

TELL YOURSELF!

I feel healthy and full of life and love.

NERVOUSNESS

Shaking legs, pounding heart,
what do I do? From where do I start?

Why be nervous, you are the best,
apologize to yourself for not believing it
and take the burden off your chest.

o SORRY, I DIDN'T TRUST YOU

o SORRY, I UNDERESTIMATED YOU

o

o

TELL YOURSELF!

I am cool, calm and collected.

Design a website that is yours,
fill it with all that you trust of life's timeless tours.

ooo

◁▷ WWW.MYSELF.COM

ABOUT ME:

WHO I'D LIKE TO MEET:

TELL YOURSELF!

Life is beautiful. I am wonderful. My present is happy. My future is bright.

ERECTILE DYSFUNCTION

The pleasure is gone—adding to the stress,
how do I get out of this mess...

If not this, then a hundred things else you can do,
be glad, be happy, look at you!

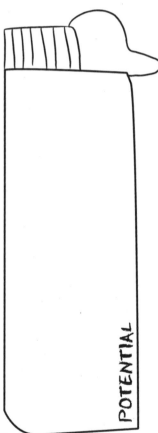

POTENTIAL

No fear restricts me. I allow the power
of my sexuality to flow
with ease and joy.

TELL YOURSEL

Given below are some of the causes of ED,
identify those that suits you and write how you will get over it.

FATIGUE / STRESS

SMOKING

PERFORMANCE ANXIETY

ALCOHOL CONSUMPTION

RELATIONSHIP ISSUES

ELL YOURSELF!

I release the anger. I don't want to hurt anyone.
I will let my feelings flow.

AMNESIA

My mind is a slate, wiped clean and blank,
my memory seems to play quite a strange prank...

If you think that your mind isn't fit,
make it here and then dare to lose it.

62

Not being able to remember things could make you queasy,
write down what you need to do—that might make things easy.

NOW

LATER

TOMORROW

SOON

ONE DAY

SOMETIME

ONCE MORE

FLU

I have fever, cough and cold,
all my works I have to put on hold.

Feeling bad about being stuck with a flu?
Don't worry, here is an app for you.

To feel fresh, don't let your garden be bare,
but keep away your allergies and well you will fare.

ASTHMA

Heaving chest, irremediable cough,
asthma has made my life very rough...

In the word search given below, you must delve,
and find the causes of asthma, given here are twelve.

```
B P E T U J M B W K S H O S C R L C G U
Z J Q I D R O X J T A E E R T S P O K F
X X V Q N Y L H E U J C Z G J M N L Z R
K V S C G Q D P J W E Q N S C J E E J Y
Z I F U M E S G S V V M F V X J C B Y L
X O A E P G P W P D V T O U T S Z K N O
U F R P G T H N A U D G C E J V T O W L
A X V C D T D B I S J R N W U I I B J G
L N F B H A I P N T I A N D V T M X G R
Z B U S D C T F T S S M A U N Q R T I
Y A V L L T Q C N T O S I L L I B Q I R
B R S E S S W P S W C O L R O Y P C D C
I L A M X A X E I B Z O L M O N F E G C
R T S C O E P V N R P O L L E N F M X U
O W S O M K Q C F Y Z V W G B N Y U E U
C Q P L D T E S C L E Z J C T L C W D K
B A Y D D S Z F I X U R V N A K G W I A
S A H A Q U U N R V N H A J P R X H O U
H Q O I M W K Q H H P A Z X C V H E L F
L N S R Y I F X Q O G D U Q Q F W N R I
```

DUST	SMOKE	PETS	FLU
COLD AIR	POLLUTION	FUMES	MOLD
GRASS	PAINT	POLLEN	PESTS

TELL YOURSELF!

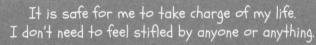

It is safe for me to take charge of my life.
I don't need to feel stifled by anyone or anything.

You need no doctor, need no quack,
write your plans to deal with an asthma attack.

YOUR ASTHMA
PLANS

TELL YOURSELF!

I am free. Nothing stops me. I can breathe.

FATIGUE

Too much work or none at all,
why am I always tired and ready to fall?

Even if it would take all your might,
get out of this maze and you will be alright.

I love my life. I love my work.
My life is rich and abundant.

TELL YOURSEL

If you are having trouble in planning your day,
make a to-do list for yourself, if you may.

To-Do List

☐ _____

☐ _____

☐ _____

☐ _____

☐ _____

☐ _____

☐ _____

☐ _____

☐ _____

☐ _____

ELL YOURSELF!

I am healthy. I am whole.
I love everything around me.

69

THYROID

A dysfunction of the butterfly-shaped gland,
leading to all kinds of issues, small and grand...

Some Yoga poses can help cure hyperthyroidism issues,
find what they are called in English, you have a few clues.

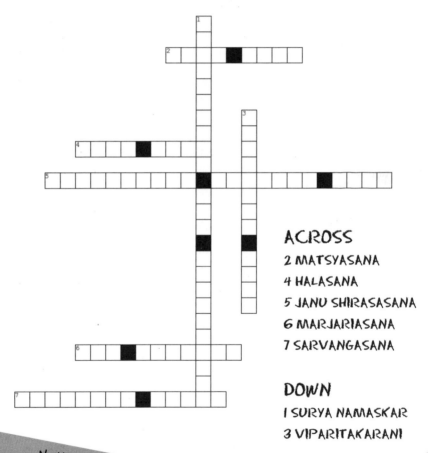

ACROSS
2 MATSYASANA
4 HALASANA
5 JANU SHIRASASANA
6 MARJARIASANA
7 SARVANGASANA

DOWN
1 SURYA NAMASKAR
3 VIPARITAKARANI

Nothing can limit me. I allow
myself to express freely.

70

Icons of human organs all across this page,
spot the thyroid gland, whatever be your age.

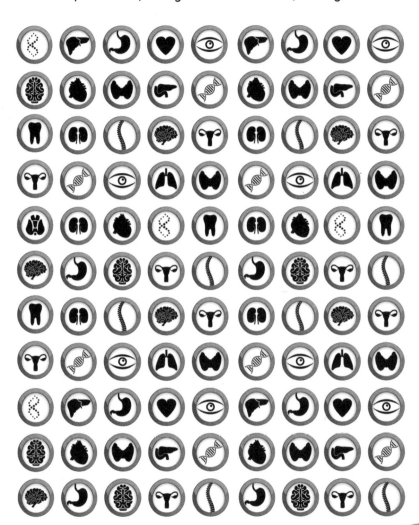

I am healthy and perfect. Nothing limits
or restricts me from doing anything.

RASH

Itching, scratching without any reason,
they appear out of nowhere, no matter what season...

Rashes can happen anytime, anywhere.
Make a poem on them, if you care.

Oops! I've got a rash
and I feel like trash.
How I wish this one I could bash
and out of my body make it dash.

What causes you an allergy?
Color if it's here. Draw, if you cannot see.

oybeans

wheat

eggs

Peanuts

MiLK

73

NAUSEA

When your stomach turns and twists,
giving you signs that it has to throw out bits...

What can some causes of nausea be,
write them here for all to see.

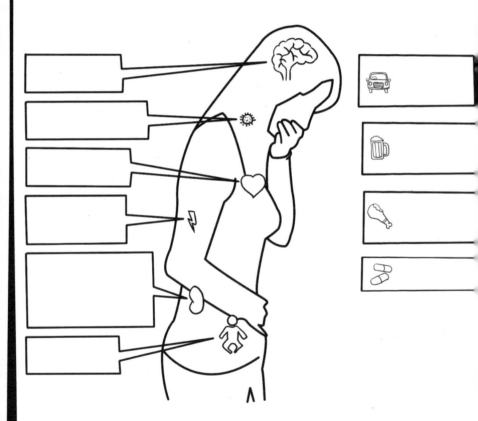

What everyone finds great but makes you nauseous,
list it here, it will be a secret between us.

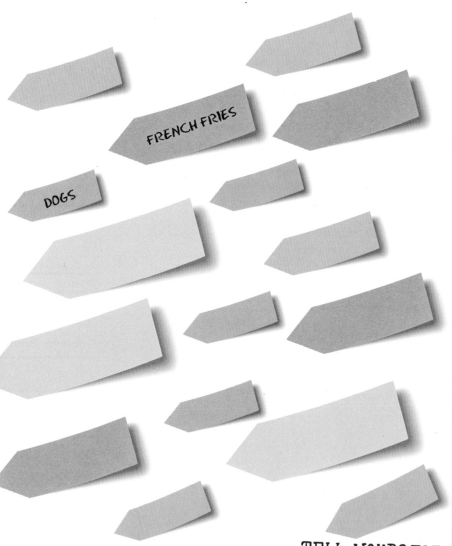

FRENCH FRIES

DOGS

TELL YOURSELF!

No one and nothing can harm me.
I am protected. I am secured.

SEIZURES

People may think it's weird and it's strange,
that your behavior is out of range...
Seizures need quick action,
label these steps
so in future,
you won't have to think about instant reaction.

....

....

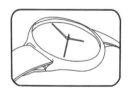  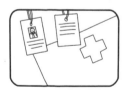

....

....

Join the dots here and there,
make any pattern—for all you care.

NAIL BITING

Mindlessly twisting your hair or biting your nails?
Is it your nervousness' trails?

What are the teeth saying to the nail?
Write fast, don't work at the pace of a snail.

TELL YOURSELF!
I have the power to control my habits. My nails and fingers are strong and healthy.

Name five things you coat your fingers with,
and get rid of nail biting forthwith?

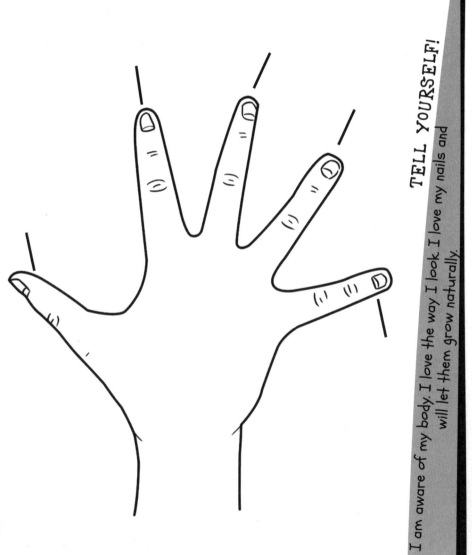

EYE PROBLEMS

You squeeze and squint and stretch your gaze,
things still seem to be in a haze...

Let's go back to class five—you ask why,
to label the parts of the eye!

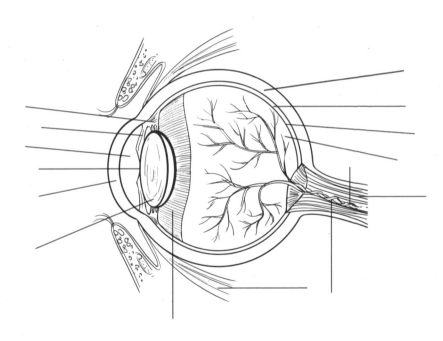

In this, there are lots of eyes,
mark the ones that are half open, be wise.

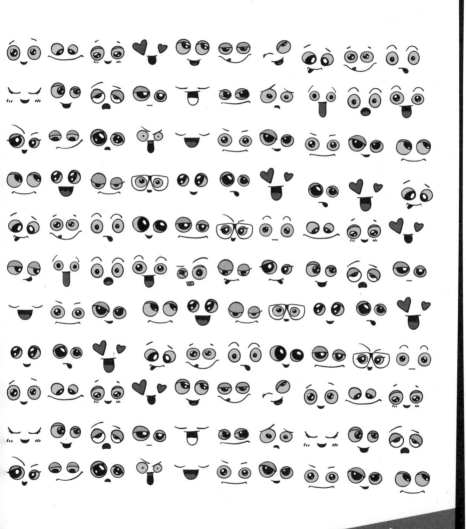

I can see the beauty of my life.
I am safe and secure.

HICCUPS

All of a sudden, your chest heaves up,
no sneeze, no cough, only a hiccup...

Hold your breath, or pinch your nose,
know of any other remedies, give us a dose!

TELL YOURSELF!
I am relaxed and centered.

Look across, down and up,
in this word cloud, find hiccup.

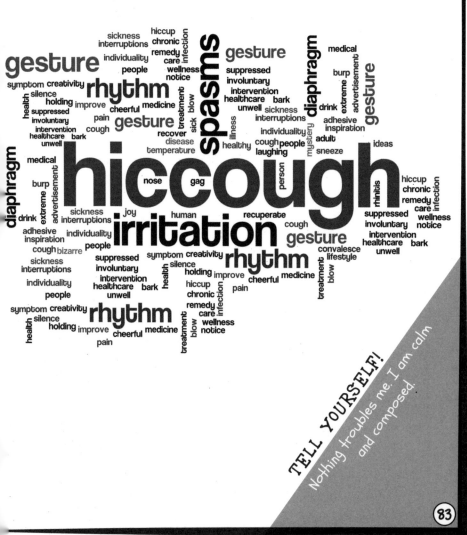

TELL YOURSELF!
Nothing troubles me. I am calm
and composed.

BODY ODOR

Coming from self or from someone else,
always a bad experience, nothing else.

What if you were in onion's place?
What would you be telling others on their face?

84

Write about three experiences that you can share, where stinking people beat you fair and square.

TELL YOURSELF!

I feel free and confident. I approve of myself.

CRYING

I cry at the drop of a hat,
have tried everything to control—this or that.

Pile up your problems here,
and knock them down without a care.

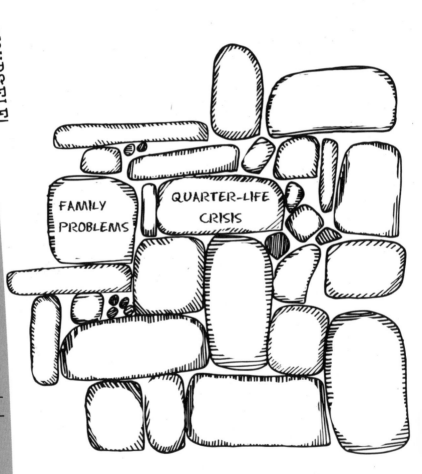

FAMILY PROBLEMS

QUARTER-LIFE CRISIS

Your eyes are the windows to the soul,
make some motivational post-its—that's the goal.

I AM STRONG.
I WON'T BREAK DOWN.

TELL YOURSELF!

I allow myself to cry and release my pains and fears. I treat myself gently.

EMOTIONAL INSTABILITY

Feelings that are too scattered,
they leave you beaten and battered...

How do you feel today?
Make it here, so your moods can stay.

DATE _____   DATE _____   DATE _____   DATE _____

DATE _____   DATE _____   DATE _____   DATE _____

DATE _____   DATE _____   DATE _____   DATE _____   DATE _____

DATE _____   DATE _____   DATE _____   DATE _____   DATE _____

Going through an emotional breakdown?
Rant, whine, abuse—pen everything down.

TELL YOURSELF!

I am strong. I am powerful.
I can recover from setbacks.

SINUSITIS

A blocked nose and a heavy head,
have you been able to leave your bed?

Something must have led to this,
can you figure out the causes of sinusitis?

I am at peace and in harmony with everyone and everything around me.

TELL YOURSEL

You have got a problem, how would you know,
It's easy, if these symptoms show.

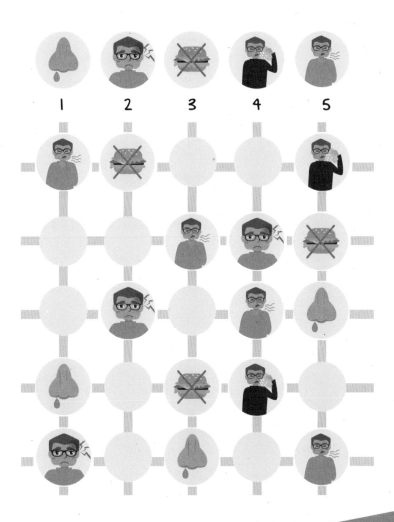

ELL YOURSELF!

People around me love me.
I am surrounded by love and goodwill.

MENOPAUSE

Ovaries going high and dry,
giving me all the problems of the world, oh why?

The seven dwarves of menopause are given here,
give them suitable names, don't just stare!

ITCHY

BITCHY

Getting hot flashes at work?
Color this scene, don't just stink.

TELL YOURSELF!

I love all the cycles of life.
I am confident and strong.

STAGE FRIGHT

Countless eyes are on you,
what you must say or do, you have no clue...

When going on stage seems a long staircase,
write one point at a time and each fear you must face.

TRY TO STAND FIRM ON YOUR FEE

I am a born performer. I thrive under pressure.

TELL YOURSELF

PANIC

PANIC

PHOBIA

STRESS

KNEE PAIN

SEA SICKNESS

ACNE

ALCOHOLISM

MIGRAINE

URINARY PROBLEMS

FROZEN SHOULDER

DENTAL ISSUES

DIABETES

ASTHMA

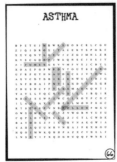

FATIGUE

THYROID

THYROID

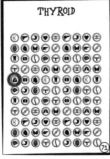

NAUSEA

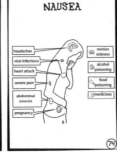

SEIZURES

EYE PROBLEMS

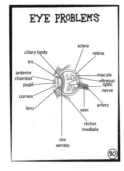

EYE PROBLEMS

HICCUPS

SINUSITIS

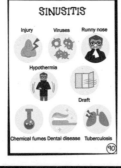

SINUSITIS